WAY Off the Church Wall

Rob Portlock

Author of
Off the Church Wall

INTERVARSITY PRESS
DOWNERS GROVE, ILLINOIS 60515

To Karen, Rick and Kristy

InterVarsity Press is the book-publishing division of InterVarsity Christian Fellowship, a student movement active on campus at hundreds of universities, colleges and schools of nursing. For information about local and regional activities, write Public Relations Dept., InterVarsity Christian Fellowship, 6400 Schroeder Rd., P.O. Box 7895, Madison, WI 53707-7895.

Distributed in Canada through InterVarsity Press, 860 Denison St., Unit 3, Markham, Ontario L3R 4H1, Canada.

Cover illustration: Rob Portlock

ISBN 0-8308-1281-4

Printed in the United States of America ∞

Library of Congress Cataloging-in-Publication Data

Portlock, Rob.
   Way off the church wall/Rob Portlock.
      p.   cm.
    ISBN 0-8308-1281-4
    1. Christian life—Caricatures and cartoons. 2. American wit and
humor, Pictorial. I. Title.
  BV4517.P57 1989
  741.5'973—dc20   89-11230
                                    CIP

18 17 16 15 14 13 12 11 10 9 8 7 6 5 4 3 2 1
99 98 97 96 95 94 93 92 91 90 89

Introduction

I still remember being floored when I found out that Charlie Chaplin had written the beautiful but sad song "Smile," which was immortalized by the one and only Nat King Cole. I could not come to grips with the idea of this comic genius writing a haunting, sad song about a broken heart.

I guess that's what interests me about humor and humorists. Somewhere along the way, like many of us, Chaplin had discovered the sad side of life. Yet through it, he was still able to look for the lighter side. As the song says, "Smile though your heart is aching; smile even though it's breaking."

God gives us reason for joy in the midst of life's hard times. I hope this book will add to that for you.

Rob Portlock

"Something tells me we're in for quite a sermon this morning."

"You've got the wrong line. This isn't St. Peter's line. It's the line to Amy Grant's Cleveland concert."

"Don't push your luck!"

"Come in, Pastor, we were expecting you."

"He put four years of sermons on computer, and then accidentally hit erase."

"Quick, call 9-1-1!"

"All right! Where did you put the church?"

"Dexter, get up, or some radical, liberal theologian is going to steal your flock!"

"If you have a minute, I'd like to tell you about the difference Jesus has made in my life."

"I should warn you. He just read *The Joyful Christian* by C. S. Lewis."

"Sure know who the big tithers are around here . . ."

"We're lucky to have such a dedicated pastor."

"Hello, this is Carol, the youth pastor. It's been one of those days, so at the beep please hang up."

"Well, what did you expect it to say?"

"It was his last request."

"What do you think? Should we pray or paddle?"

"I wonder what this will do to our pension plan!"

"Yes! I am a Christian! How did you know?"

"It's the last time I fill out a Visitor's Card!"

"They do it every time he finishes his sermon by noon."

"Poor Solomon, he never seems to have anything decent to wear."

"Walter, come down from there this minute or that's the last book on the rapture I get you!"

YOUTH PASTOR

MASTERS
DEGREE
YOUTH PSYCHOLOGY

DOCTORATE
YOUTH EDUCATION

BACHELOR
OF ARTS
YOUTH BEHAVIOR

SCHOOL OF THEOLOGY
YOUTH MINISTRY

PORTLESK

"Pastor Smith has invited you up here so he can have a chance to stare at you!"

"How can I be sure this is inerrant?"

"Looks like the new pastor has met everyone."

"I wish the new youth pastor didn't feel he had to entertain us so much."

"I think it's time we talk about the congregation's attention span."

"All those in favor of blaming all the church's problems on the youth pastor say, 'Yea.'"

"I don't think the pastor's going to change his mind on this subject."

The day Susan forgot and yawned during her husband's sermon.

"And now, here's our speaker with an inspirational word about our lack of tithing of late."

The properly equipped youth pastor's office

"It's our new Benediction Pulpit."

"My sermon today is 'Overcoming Shyness.'"

"You can come out now! The offering's over!"

"God told me last night if you didn't buy me a bike before summer, he'd make you go bald."

"It's certain to please you and your husband, and it's on the acceptable list given to us by your church's Women's Auxiliary Group."

"Ted, I'm 29 and from Des Moines, Iowa. I've been a youth pastor for three years. I'm totally broke, and if I don't win here today I'll be living in my car."

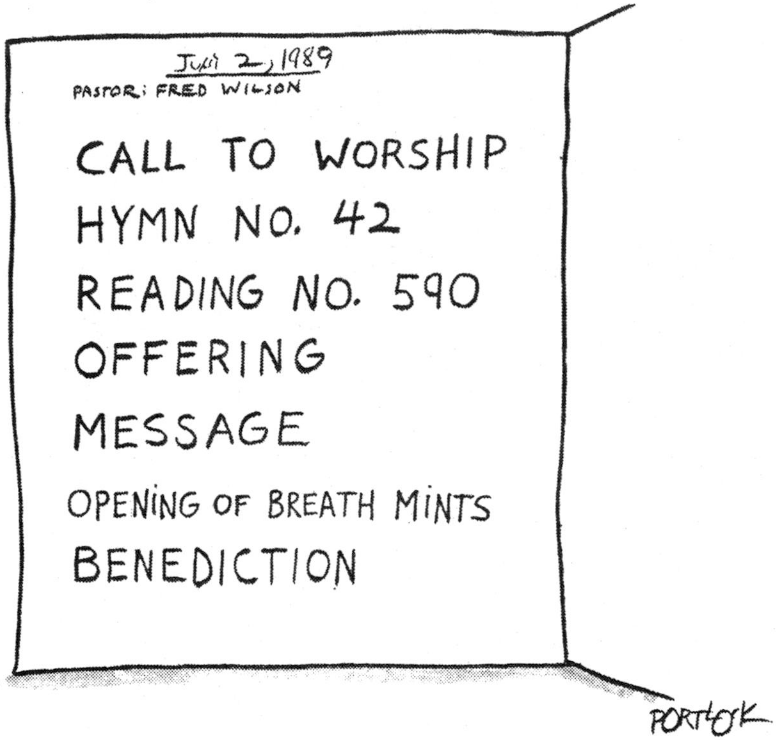
July 2, 1989
PASTOR: FRED WILSON
CALL TO WORSHIP
HYMN NO. 42
READING NO. 590
OFFERING
MESSAGE
OPENING OF BREATH MINTS
BENEDICTION
PORTLOCK

"Is this the day you take the youth group to Disneyland?"

Mrs. Riley forgets to check the volume control and catches Pastor Smith off guard.

"Bobby, I just think you're too sensitive . . ."

"I've created the perfect assistant."

"Okay, okay! I take it back. It wasn't a bad sermon!"

"Our last pastor's wife's shoes . . . can you fill 'em?"

PORTLOCK

"Grace, sit down! You're not the 'God's Grace' the pastor's talking about!"

"For crying out loud, Harry, relax!"

"And to those who didn't give to the church fund . . . good luck!"

"Yes, I am a pastor! How did you know?"

"I for one think it's time to propose to the board that we upgrade our youth transportation!"

"So how did you like my sermon today?"

PORTLOCK

Cable Church

"I think he's missing the whole point!"

"I heard you had a unique way of sizing up new pastors' wives."

"Ever since we started selling VCRs, our Sunday-morning attendance has increased twenty per cent!"

"... And now we'll wait a moment while the Love Choir decides which song they'll sing."

"Now, what was that wisecrack you made about dentists in your sermon last week?"

"It's becoming a contest to see who finds the Scripture first."

"I still say the new pastor is trying too hard to please everyone!"

"Can't you get it through your head, Riley? You don't have to hand out tracts here!"

"Since no volunteers came forward, I'd like to now introduce the Westside Church Inflate-o-Choir."

QUESTION:
WHICH ONE OF THESE DOES
A PASTOR'S WIFE FEEL LIKE
WHEN COMING TO A NEW CHURCH?

PORTLOCK

"Harold's finally found a place for his quiet time."

"Tough interview?"

"Somehow I thought it would be different."

Christian entrepreneurship is born.

"I said you should have a three-day crusade but nooooo, you had to have seven!"

"I like to think of myself as the facilitator and enabler of this church rather than the senior pastor or chief executive officer."

"Our speaker today is a missionary from Africa, here to tell us about his adventures in the Congo."

"Looks like no church today, eh, Mabel?"

"I know you're just trying to be a good youth pastor, but this is going too far!"

"I don't care if it *is* the armor of God. You take it off or go sleep on the couch."

"And our guest speaker is perhaps best known for his fabulously successful, nationwide seminars on 'humility' . . ."

"I think the pastor's entrances are getting out of hand!"

"Kids: Don't try this at home."

"Thanks for the marriage counseling, Pastor. We feel much better."

"... and whatever you do, Harry, don't demand to get everything that's coming to you!"